Decodable Readers

Take-Home Blackline Masters

Grade 1, Volume 1

HOUGHTON MIFFLIN HARCOURT
School Publishers

Photo credits

Unit 1

Cover © HMH/Ken Karp Photography, title page © Rob & SAS/Corbis, **19** © LWA-Dan Tardiff/Corbis, **20** Blend Images/Alamy, **21** Adrian Brockwell/Alamy, **22** John Rowley/Getty Images, **23** Doug Menuez/Photo Disc/Getty Images, **24** Sean Justice/Corbis, **35** Image Source/Corbis, **36** Chuck Franklin/Alamy, **37** Comstock/Corbis, **38** David Young-Wolff/PhotoEdit, **39** Rob & SAS/Corbis, **40** Photo Disc, **75** Scott Wohrman/Corbis, **76** Digital Vision/Alamy, **77** Corbis/Superstock, **78** JupiterImages/Comstock/Alamy, **79** Image Source/Corbis, **80** Moodboard/Corbis, **81** Scott Wohrman/Corbis. All other photos are property of Houghton Mifflin Harcourt.

Unit 2

Cover George Doyle, Title Stockbyte/Getty Images, **19** © Philip Mugridge / Alamy, **20** © Tracy Hebden / Alamy, **21** © Peter Arnold, Inc. / Alamy, **22** © Corbis, **23** © Gary Salter / zefa / Corbis, **24** © Eric and David Hosking/CORBIS, **51** © B.A.E. Inc. / Alamy, **52** © Wim Wiskerke / Alamy, **53** © Jupiterimages/ Thinkstock / Alamy, **54** © Jill Stephenson / Alamy, **55** © Jupiterimages/ Creatas / Alamy, **56** © Juiterimages/ BananaStock / Alamy, **75** Brand X Pictures, **76** ©1998 EyeWire, Inc./Getty Images, **77** © Blend Images / Alamy, **78** © Vario Images GmbH & Co.KG / Alamy, **79** Blend Images / SuperStock, **80** Stockbyte/Getty Images, **81** Brand X Pictures, **97** © Mike Harrington / Alamy, **99** © i love images / Alamy, **100** © PhotoAlto / Alamy, **101** © Clare Charleson / Alamy, **102** Artville, **103** © Nick Hanna / Alamy, **104** © AM Corporation / Alamy. All other photos are property of Houghton Mifflin Harcourt.

Unit 3

Cover Alaska Stock LLC/Alamy, **Title page** Getty Images/DAJ, **19** Alejandro Balaguer / Getty Images **20** © Dan Guravich/CORBIS **21** © Sanford / Agliolo / CORBIS **22** © Tim Wright / CORBIS **23** © Arco Images / Alamy **24** © Robert C. Paulson / Alamy **43** DAJ / Getty Images **44** © Bart Harris / Alamy **45** © Westend 61 / Alamy **46** © George McCarthy / CORBIS **47** Peter Lilja / age fotostock / Superstock **48** Norbert Rosing / National Geographic / Getty Images **107** © Cal Vornberger / Photo Researchers, Inc. **108** © Cal Vornberger / Photo Researchers, Inc. **109** Ron Rothschadl/US Fish and Wildlife Service. **110** © Cal Vornberger / Photo Researchers, Inc. **111** © Cal Vornberger / Photo Researchers, Inc. **112** © Cal Vornberger / Photo Researchers, Inc. All other photos are property of Houghton Mifflin Harcourt.

ISBN 978-0-547-29635-7

1 2 3 4 5 6 7 8 9 0928 17 16 15 14 13 12 11 10
4500255654   ^ B C D E F G

Unit 1
Around the Neighborhood

Contents

TEKS **1.3A** decode words in context and in isolation; **1.3C(i)** decode using closed syllables; **1.3H** identify/read high-frequency words

Phonics

Words with Short <u>a</u> Read each sentence. Then point to and read words with the short <u>a</u> sound. Tell which picture the sentence is about.

Dan sat.

I am a cat.

2

Dan and Nan

by Evan MacDonald

illustrated by Lorinda Bryan Cauley

I am Dan Cat.

3

Dan Cat sat.

TEKS 1.1B identify upper- and lower-case letters: 1.21B(iii) capitalize names of people

Letters   Read Together

Names   A name begins with a capital letter. Read the names. Say the letters in each name.

Dan

Nan

Write your name. Say each letter. Which letter is a capital letter? Name the lower-case letters.

Dan and Nan can play.

I am Nan Cat.

8

Nan Cat sat.

Dan sat. Nan sat.

6

7

TEKS 1.3A decode words in isolation; 1.3B apply letter-sound knowledge to create words; 1.3C(i) decode using closed syllables

Phonics

Words with Short **a** Read these words.

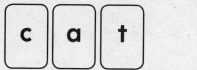

| c | a | t |

| s | a | t |

Read the words on the path.

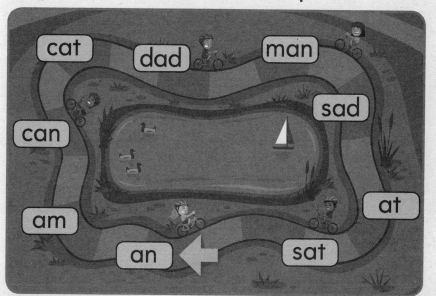

10

7A

Nat Cat

by Uta Tibi
illustrated by Noah Jones

Nat Cat sat.

11

Nan sat.

TEKS 1.3H identify/read high-frequency words; 1.3I monitor decoding accuracy; 1.5 read aloud with fluency/comprehension ELPS 4A learn English sound-letter relationships/decode

Fluency  Read Together

Words to Know You have to remember some words. Read these words.

| play | with | and |

Letter-Sounds Letter-sounds can help you read other words. Read these names.

| Nan | Tad | Nat |

Read Aloud Work with a partner. Take turns reading aloud "Nat Cat." Help each other read words correctly.

Nan, Tad, and Nat can play.

Tad sat.

16

13

Nan can play with Tad.

Nat! Nat! Nat Cat!

14

15

TEKS **1.3A** decode words in context and in isolation; **1.3C(i)** decode using closed syllables; **1.3H** identify/read high-frequency words

Phonics

Words with Short <u>a</u> Read the sentences. Then point to and read words with the short <u>a</u> sound. Name the girl and her pet in the pictures.

Fan can nap.

Pam can play.

18

13A

14A

Fan, Fan, Fan
by Graham Neu

Pat sat. Pat can be a fan.
Fan, fan, fan, fan.

19

15A

Dan sat. Dan can be a fan.
Fan, fan, fan, fan.

16A

TEKS 1.17A generate ideas for writing; **1.17E** publish/share writing **ELPS 5B** write using new basic/content-based vocabulary

Writing *Read Together*

Plan Are you a fan? What activity do you love to watch?

Write Draw a picture. Write about the picture. You can use these sentences: **I like** _____.
I am a big fan. Share your work with classmates.

Can you be a fan?
Fan! Fan! Fan! Fan!

Nan sat. Nan can be a fan.
Fan, fan, fan, fan.

Sam sat. Sam can be a fan.
Fan, fan! Fan, fan!

Pam sat. Pam can be a fan.
Fan, fan! Fan, fan!

18A

TEKS **1.3A** decode words in context and in isolation; **1.3C(i)** decode using closed syllables; **1.3H** identify/read high-frequency words

Phonics

Words with Short i Read each riddle. Find the picture that answers it. Point to and read the short i words.

It has a fin. What is it?

Sid can hit it. What is it?

A cat can rip it. What is it?

26

20A

Can It Fit?

by Chandra Majors

illustrated by Elizabeth Allen

It is a tan cap.

What can fit in it?

27

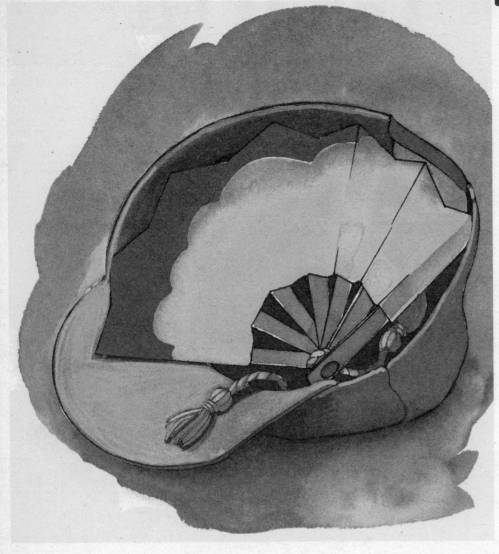

A fan can fit in it.
Is it for a fan?

Fluency

Punctuation Marks Read these sentences. Each sentence should sound different. Use the end marks to help you.

Can it fit?
It can fit.
It can fit!

Read Aloud Work with a partner. Use end marks to help you read aloud "Can It Fit?"

Look at Sam!

It is his cap.

Ram is his cat.

32

A tin pan is in it.

Is it for a tin pan?

29

A map can fit in it.
Is it for a map?

Ram Cat can sit in it.
Is it for Ram Cat?

Phonics

Words with Short i Read the words on each ladder. Tell which words have the short i sound.

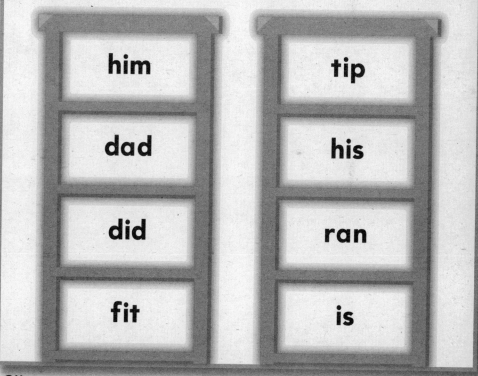

him	tip
dad	his
did	ran
fit	is

34

I Ran

by Chris Gericho

Pam ran.

Tif did, too.

35

Dad is with Pat.

Dad ran. Pat ran.

TEKS 1.28 share information/ideas by speaking clearly ELPS 3E share information in cooperative learning interactions

Speaking

Read Together

Share Think about these questions:

- When do you run?
- Do you like to run?

Tell a partner about running. Use these tips.

Speaking Tips

- Speak clearly and loudly enough to be heard.
- Do not speak too fast or too slowly.

I ran, ran, ran!
Did you?

40

Sid ran, ran, ran.
Tip is with him.

37

29A

Look at Tim.

Tim ran. Nan did, too.

Dan ran, ran, ran!

Tam ran. Cam did, too.

30A

TEKS **1.3A** decode words in context and in isolation; **1.3C(i)** decode using closed syllables; **1.3H** identify/read high-frequency words

Phonics

Words with Short i Read the clues. Tell which pet each clue is about. Point to and read the short i words.

It is big and can sit.

It is little and can dig.

42

31A

32A

Pam

by Tony Manero

illustrated by Jeff Shelly

Tip has a bat.

It is for Pam.

43

Did Pam bat?

Pam sat!

TEKS **1.3A(i)** decode words with consonants; **1.1B** identify upper- and lower-case letters; **1.21B(iii)** capitalize names of people; **ELPS 4A** learn English sound-letter relationships/decode

Letters

Identify Names

| Tip | cap | Pam | bat | Rip |

1. Point to and read three names. What kind of letter do they begin with?
2. Point to and read the word that ends with **t**. Is it a name? How do you know?
3. Read each word. Which words are names and which are not? How do you know?

34A

Bam! Pam did it!
It is a big, big hit!

Rip has a cap.
It is for Pam.

48

45

35A

Pam has a cap!
Pam has a bat, too.

Pam is at bat.
Can Pam hit it?

46

47

36A

Phonics

Words with Short o Read each word. Then use the words in sentences. Try to use two or more words in one sentence.

| mop | top | pot |
| box | log | hop |

50

38A

Lil and Max

by Alexis Davis

illustrated by Akemi Gutierrez

Lil got a big, big mop.
Can Lil and Max sit on top?

51

Can they do it? No!

TEKS 1.3A(ii) decode words with vowels; 1.3D decode words with common spelling patterns; 1.6D categorize words   ELPS 4A learn English sound-letter relationships/decode

Spelling Patterns

Read Together

Sort Words Read these words. How are they alike?

| mop   fox   got   pot   hop   box |

Copy this chart. Write two words in each column. Read the words again. How are the words in each column alike?

_op	_ot	_ox

Lil can sit on top!

Max can sit on top, too!

Max got a big, big pot.

Can Lil and Max hop on it?

56

53

Hip, hop. Hip, hop, hop.
Lil and Max hop in it!

Lil and Max find a cot.
It is a big, big, BIG cot!

54

55

TEKS **1.3A** decode words in context and in isolation; **1.3C(i)** decode using closed syllables; **1.3H** identify/read high-frequency words

Phonics

Words with Short o Read each question and answer it. Then point to and read words with the short o sound.

Can the dog fit in the box?

Can the dog sit on the box?

Can the dog fix the box?

58

Did Dix Dog Do It?

by Oliver Berry
illustrated by Mike Gordon

Dad Dog is sad.
Dad has to fix it.
Did Dix Dog do it?

59

Sal Dog is sad.
Did Dix Dog do it?

Book Information

Book Parts The arrows point to the title, the name of the author, and the name of the illustrator.

title —→
author
illustrator

What do you like about the author's words? What do you like about the illustrator's art?

No! Max Cat did it!

64

Mom Dog is sad.
It is not funny!
Did Dix Dog do it?

61

47A

Lon Dog is sad.
Did Dix Dog do it?

Doc Dog is sad.
Did Dix Dog do it?

62

63

48A

TEKS **1.3A** decode words in context; **1.3C(i)** decode using closed syllables; **1.3E** read words with inflectional endings; **1.3H** identify/read high-frequency words

Phonics

Words that End with -s Read each sentence pair. Which is Rob? Which is Pam?

Rob can hop.   **Pam can dig.**

Rob hops a lot. **Pam digs a lot.**

66

Is It Funny?

by Laurence Christopher

illustrated by Liz Callen

Pat can tap.

Pat taps, taps, taps.

67

51A

Hal is not sad.
Hal sits in his box.

TEKS 1.3A(ii) decode words with vowels; 1.6A identify nouns/verbs ELPS 1C use strategic learning techniques to acquire vocabulary; 4A learn English sound-letter relationships/decode

Vocabulary 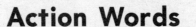 Read Together

Action Words

| tap | sit | fan | hop | mix |

Act It Out Work with a partner. Read the words. Then write each word on a card. Place the cards face-down. Pick a card and act out the word. See if your partner can guess the word. Then have your partner act out a word and you try to guess the action.

Hal has a pad.
What is on it?
It is funny!

72

Ron Dog is hot.
Pat fans the hot dog.

69

53A

Hal can sing.

Hal sings a rap.

Pat has a big pot.

Pat can mix a lot.

TEKS **1.3A** decode words in isolation; **1.3B** apply letter-sound knowledge to create words; **1.3C(i)** decode using closed syllables

Phonics

Words with Short e Read these words.

Read the words on the path. Tell which words have the short e sound.

74

56A

Pals

by Aiden Brandt

Len and his pals can hop!
Len led all his pals.

75

Lin has a pet dog.
Wags is a good pal!

Unit 1/Lesson 4/Selection 1

Words in Print

Read Together

Speech Print can show what people say. Look at the photo. In the story, Len and his pals hop. Read what Len is saying.

My pals and I can all hop.

Draw and Write Draw a picture of yourself talking to a friend. Write what you say.

Ted sat on a big log.
Ted sat with his pals.

Wes let his pals in.
His pals can play in his den.

80

77

59A

Can Mom be a pal?
Yes! Mom and Ben get logs.

Six pals ran six laps.
Who led the pals? Mel did!

78

79

60A

TEKS **1.3A** decode words in isolation; **1.3C(i)** decode using closed syllables

Phonics

Words with Short e Read the words. Find three short e words in a row. Read those words again.

sat	wig	pet
bed	yes	ten
win	get	his

82

62A

Ned

by David McCoy

illustrated by Neena Chawla

Here is Ned.
Who is he?

83

Ned is not Ned Pig.
Ned is not Ned Ox.
Ned is Ned Hog.

64A

TEKS 1.1B identify upper- and lower-case letters; 1.21B(i) capitalize beginning of sentences; 1.21B(iii) capitalize names of people

Letters

Read Together

Identify Letters Names begin with a capital letter. Sentences begin with a capital letter, too. Here is a sentence about Ned Hog:

Can Ned Hog get a big hit?

Which words begin with capital letters? Which are names? What word begins the sentence? Why does the word *hit* begin with a lower-case letter?

Who is Ned Hog?

Ned is top hog!

Ned wins, wins, wins!

Is Ned Hog big? Yes!

Does Ned have ten wigs?   No!

Ned Hog has ten hats!

88

85

Ned has a cap, too.
Ned Hog is at bat.
Can he get a big hit? Yes!

Ned Hog is hot.
It is not hot in here.
Ned can nap in his bed.

TEKS **1.3A** decode words in context and in isolation; **1.3C(i)** decode using closed syllables; **1.3H** identify/read high-frequency words

Phonics

Words with Short e Read each sentence. Point to and reread the short e words. Then tell which picture matches each sentence.

Vic gets his jet.
Ken has a pen.

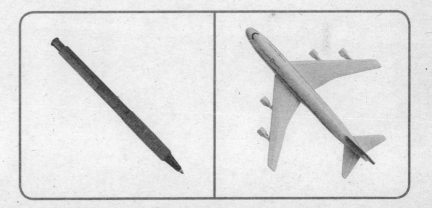

90

68A

My Pets

by Alice Ling

illustrated by Meryl Treatner

Big Vic is my pet dog.

Kit is my pet cat.

91

Kit can get six red jets.
Get the jets, Kit!

TEKS 1.27A listen attentively/ask relevant questions; 1.29 follow discussion rules ELPS 2I
demonstrate listening comprehension of spoken English

Listening

Listen for information Join a small group. Take turns talking about pets you have or would like to have. Use the tips.

Listening Tips

- Look at the person who is talking.
- Listen carefully to hear the information.
- Raise your hand to ask a question or to speak.

70A

Kit fits in the cat bed.

Big Vic does not fit in it.

Big Vic does not fit in my bed!

Big Vic can get ten tin men.

Here, Big Vic. Get set. Go!

96

93

Kit and Big Vic nap in the den.
Kit and Big Vic nap with me.

Big Vic and Kit get fed.
Sit, Big Vic, sit!

94

95

TEKS **1.3A** decode words in context and in isolation; **1.3C(i)** decode using closed syllables; **1.3H** identify/read high-frequency words

Phonics

Words with Short <u>u</u> Read and answer each question. Then point to and read the short <u>u</u> words.

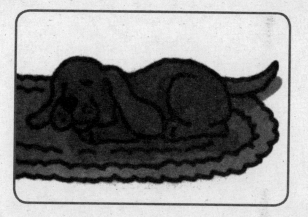

Is the pup up on a bed?   yes no

Is the pup on a bus?   yes no

Is the pup on a rug?   yes no

98

74A

Fun in the Sun

by Norman Swaderski
illustrated by Stephen Lewis

Jen Pig is hot.
Can Jen hop in? No!

75A

99

Ed Hog is hot.
Can Ed hop in? Yes!
Ed has fun, fun, fun!

100

Decoding

Read Together

Read Carefully   Read this story.

> The sun is up. Jen is hot. Can Ed get Jen in the mud? Yes! Ed and Jen can play in the mud!

Think   Do you think you read every word correctly? How do you know? If a word is hard to read, how can you figure it out? Reread the story.

105

Ed has fun in the sun.
Jen has fun in the sun, too!

Ed pulls his friend.
Tug, tug. Hold on, Jen.

104

101

77A

Can Jen hop in? Yes!
Jen has fun, fun, fun!

Ed Hog hops up, up, up!
Jen Pig hops up, up, up!

102

103

TEKS 1.3A decode words in isolation; **1.3C(i)** decode using closed syllables

Phonics

Words with Short <u>u</u> Read each word. Then use the words in sentences. Use two or more words in one sentence.

sun	up	rug
pup	bug	bun

Yams! Yum!

by Rona Blanca

illustrated by Gina Freschet

Yak is in bed,
but he has to get up.

107

Yak has to get yams.
What can Yak do?

TEKS **1.1A** recognize that print represents speech; **1.19A** write brief compositions **ELPS 5A** use English sound-letter relationships to write

Words in Print

Read Together

Speech Remember that print can show what people say. Look at the picture. Read what Yak says about yams.

I can fit ten big, fat yams in my red bag.

Draw and Write Draw yourself talking to a family member about your favorite food. Write what you say.

Yak has his yams.
He has lots and lots.
Yams! Yum, yum, yum!

Can Yak get big, fat yams?
Yes! He can get lots and lots.

112

109

83A

Yak can set his yams in a bag.
His red bag can hold lots!

Yak can fit ten yams in his bag.
His bag is full. Yams! Yum!

110

TEKS 1.3A decode words in isolation; **1.3C(i)** decode using closed syllables

Phonics

Words with Short <u>u</u> Read all the words. Then find three short <u>u</u> words in a row. Read those words again.

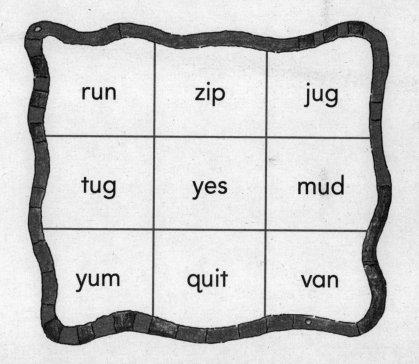

run	zip	jug
tug	yes	mud
yum	quit	van

114

Bud

by David McCoy

illustrated by Jeffrey Ebbeler

Bud is a pug. Bud is a pup.
Bud can fit in a big cup!

115

Bud digs in the mud.
Quit it, Bud! Quit it!

88A

Words

Read Together

High-Frequency Words With a partner, write each of these words on two cards:

> good   many   play   help   with

Word Game Lay the cards upside down on a table. Take turns choosing two cards. Read the words. If they match, keep them. If they don't, put them back. Who can make the most matches?

Bud can tug. Bud can run.
Bud has fun in the hot sun.
Good dog, Bud!

120

Zip! Bud hops in the tub.
Rub, rub! Rub-a-dub-dub!
Bud has fun!

117

Bud sits with us.
We play. Bud naps.

Bud can help us.
Bud gets many hugs!

Unit 2
Sharing Time

Contents

TEKS **1.3A** decode words in context and in isolation; **1.3C(i)** decode using closed syllables

Phonics

Words with Double Consonants and <u>ck</u> Read each sentence. Tell which picture it goes with. Then point to and read each name.

Jack will pack a sack.

Zack will pack hats.

Max will pack socks.

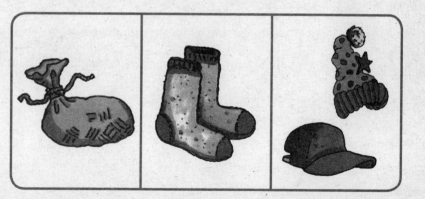

2

Ann Packs

by Ellen Catala

illustrated by Diane Paterson

"I miss Ann. I can call Ann.
Ann can come here," said Nan.

3

"Yes," said Ann. "I will come.

I will be quick, Nan."

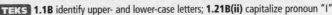

Capitalization

Read Together

Pronoun I   When **I** is a word, it is written with a capital letter. Read these sentences.

> Can I call Ann?
>
> Ann said, "I will come."
>
> I will pack six hats.

Find the letter **i**. When is it a lower-case letter? When is it a capital letter? Write a sentence about yourself using **I**.

Ann has hats and socks.

Ann has ducks and dolls.

Ann has ten big hugs for Nan.

Quick, quick, quick!

Ann will pack a big red bag.

8

5

Ann will pack ten hats.

Ann will pack ten socks.

Pack, pack, pack, pack.

Ann will pack six ducks.

Ann will pack ten dolls.

Pack, pack, pack, pack.

6

7

TEKS **1.3A** decode words in isolation; **1.3C(i)** decode using closed syllables; **1.3E** read words with inflectional endings

Phonics

Words with Double Consonants and <u>ck</u>
Read the words to go up and down the hill. Use two or more of the words in a sentence.

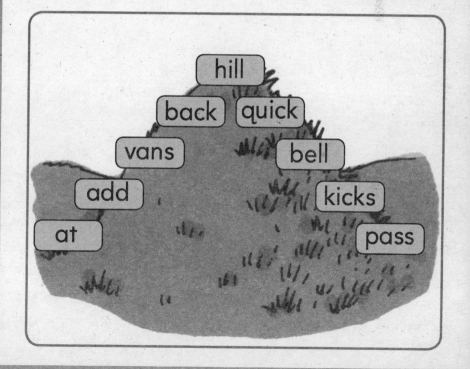

10

Tess and Jack

by Timothy Bern

illustrated by Marsha Winborn

"Call me," said Tess.
"Call me," said Jack.

11

Tess is sick. Tess is sick in bed.
Tess cannot play, but Tess can
call Jack.

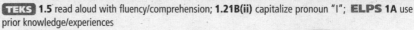

Fluency Read Together

Expression Read "Tess and Jack" aloud with a partner. Take turns on each page. Use your feelings to help you read with expression.

Pronoun I Find the letter **i** in the story. When is it a capital letter? Tell why.

Will Jack call Tess?
Yes! Yes! Jack will.
Will Tess call Jack?
Yes! Yes! Tess will.

Jack is sick. Jack is sick in bed.
Jack cannot play, but Jack can
call Tess.

16

13

11B

Tess is well. Tess is back. Tess can play. Jack is well. Jack is back. Jack can play. Tess and Jack can bat.

"I will get a mitt," said Tess. "I will get a bat," said Jack. "Hit it, Jack," said Tess. "Quick! Hit it. Get a run."

14

15

TEKS **1.3A** decode words in isolation; **1.3C(i)** decode using closed syllables

Phonics

Words with Double Consonants and <u>ck</u>

Read all the words. Find three words with <u>ck</u> in a row. Read those words again.

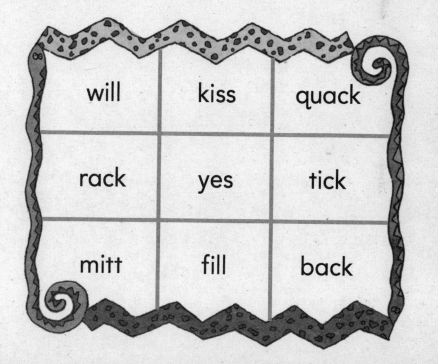

will	kiss	quack
rack	yes	tick
mitt	fill	back

18

Ducks Quack

by Kyle Stenovich

Look up at the ducks.
Quack, quack, quack.
Hear the ducks quack.

19

Look at the ducks.
Ducks can see rocks and mud.
Ducks will nip. Ducks will peck.

TEKS **1.23A** generate topics/ formulate questions; **1.23B** determine relevant sources of information
ELPS 3E share information in cooperative learning interactions

Research

Read Together

Share What You Know

Discuss with a partner what you know about ducks.

Questions   What would you like to learn about ducks? With your partner, write some questions you have about ducks. Tell how you could find answers to these questions.

Hear the duck on the hill.
Every duck can quack.
Quack, quack, quack.

Ducks will go in.
Ducks will get wet.
Ducks will quack.
Quack, quack, quack.

24

21

17B

Look at the ducks.

Ducks will dip in.

Dip, dip, dip.

Ducks will pop back up.

Pop, pop, pop.

22

23

Phonics

Words with Consonant Clusters with r Read the words. What is the second letter in each word? Read the words again. Listen for the sound for r.

26

20B

Brad and Cris

by Teresa Bashin

illustrated by Marsha Winborn

Brad Frog is red. Brad has tan
dots. Brad is red and tan.

27

Brad has a pal. His pal is Cris. Cris Frog is tan. Cris has no dots. Cris is tan and red.

Book Information

Read Together

Book Parts Point to the parts of a book.

title

author

illustrator

The **title** is the name of the story. The **author** is the person who wrote the story. The **illustrator** is the person who drew the pictures.

22B

"Look, Brad!" Cris said. "Bugs,
bugs, bugs! Grubs, grubs, grubs!
Yum!"

32

"We will go on a trip, Cris,"
Brad said. "It will be fun."
Brad did not tell Cris why.

29

Brad led Cris. Brad and Cris
hop on pads. Hop, hop! Hop,
hop, hop!

"Can we get some bugs and
grubs?" said Cris.
"Not yet," said Brad. "Not yet."

30

31

TEKS 1.3A decode words in context and in isolation; **1.3C(i)** decode using closed syllables; **1.3E** read words with inflectional endings

Phonics

Words with Consonant Clusters with r

Read the words in the box. Read the sentences. Use the words to complete the sentences.

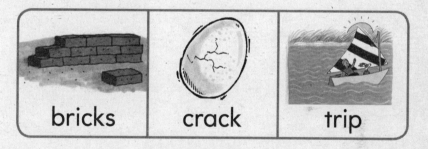

bricks	crack	trip

1. Gram and Fran go on a ____.

2. Brad fills his truck with ____.

3. The eggs drop and ____!

34

What Did Dad Get?

by Ed Floyd

illustrated by Julia Gorton

Fred has a big bag. Gram has a tan cap. It is for Dad.

35

Fred can hold up the bag. Gram will drop the tan cap in it. Pop!

TEKS 1.17A generate ideas for writing; 1.17E publish/share writing; 1.18A write brief stories

Writing

 Read Together

Plan Think about a gift you have given someone. Draw a picture of it. Then discuss it with a partner.

Write and Share Write a short story with your partner about giving gifts. Share it with the class.

Dad has his tan cap. Dad has a
red frog on top of his cap. Fred,
Jill, and Gram grin at Dad.

Jill can get the bag. Jill has an
animal. It is a red frog!

40

37

Pop! Jill drops the red frog in the bag. It is for Dad.

"Gram," said Fred, "Dad has a red frog. How did Dad get it?"

38

39

30B

TEKS 1.3A decode words in isolation; 1.3C(i) decode using closed syllables

Phonics

Words with Consonant Clusters with r Read the first word. Say the words that name the pictures. Tell which word rhymes with the first word. Write the two rhyming words on paper.

trick			
grip			
press			

42

32B

The Big Job

by Pamela Chin

illustrated by John Ceballos

Dad has a job. Dad will go to his job. Sid has a job. Sid will go to his job.

43

Dad has a big red truck.
Dad will lug bricks in his truck.

34B

Use Strategies Read Together

Read for Understanding Reread **The Big Job** on pages 43–48 carefully.

Correct and Adjust As you read the story, you might not understand a part of it. Do one or more of these things to help you:

- Reread it aloud.
- Picture in your mind what it is about.
- Think about what you already know about jobs people do using trucks.
- Ask yourself a question about the meaning, such as **What does Dad do with the bricks?**

Dad is back with Sid.
Why will Sid sit with Dad?
Dad and Sid will play!

48

Sid has a red truck. Sid will drop
his bricks on the grass.

45

Dad will dig up lots of rocks.
Dig, dig, dig, Dad!

Sid will dig up lots of rocks.
Dig, dig, dig, Sid!

TEKS **1.3A** decode words in isolation; **1.3C(i)** decode using closed syllables; **1.3D** decode words with common spelling patterns

Phonics

Words with Consonant Clusters with l Read the words on the flags. Use two or more words in a sentence.

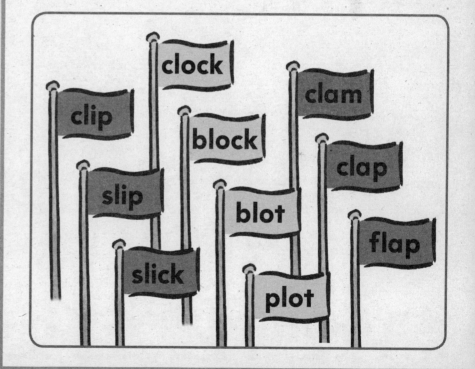

50

38B

Our Flag
by Susan Crowton

Up, up, up. The flag is on top.
It can flap. It can flip.

51

Up, up, up. The flag is on top.
It can flip. It can flap.

Unit 2/Lesson 8/Selection 1

Connections

Read Together

Make a Flag Think of what you learned about flags from the story "Our Flag." Think about flags you have seen.

Draw your own flag. Tell a partner why you like your flag. Where would you like to fly your flag?

Flags, flags, flags. Pam has a flag. She is glad she has it.

Our club has a big flag. We will sing. We will clap.

56

53

The flag is big. It is flat. They hold it up, up, up. They will not let it drop.

Flags can flip. Flags can flap. Kids hold flags up, up, up. Flags flap. Flags flip.

54

55

42B

TEKS **1.3A** decode words in isolation; **1.3C(i)** decode using closed syllables; **1.3D** decode words with common spelling patterns

Phonics

Words with Consonant Clusters with l These words are mixed up. Read the words. Write all the words with short o in one list. Write words with other vowels in another list. Read each list.

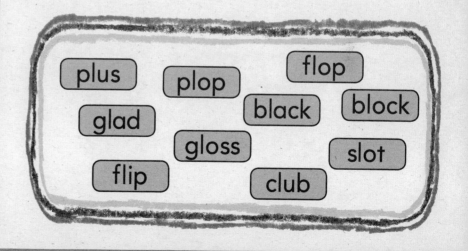

plus
plop
flop
glad
black
block
gloss
slot
flip
club

58

44B

The Plan

by Martin Avalong

illustrated by Linda Bronson

Hen has a plan. Cluck, cluck, cluck. Hen will tell it to Duck. Run, Hen! Run, run!

59

45B

Did Duck like her plan? Yes, yes, yes! Duck flaps, flaps, flaps. Duck claps, claps, claps. Hen and Duck will play today.

Decoding

Read Carefully Read this story.

> A bug nips. Hen flaps.
> The bug flips and
> zips and nips.
> Hen slaps.
> The bug quits and Hen flops.

Think Do you think you read every word correctly? If a word is hard to read, how can you figure it out? Reread the story.

Hen quits. Duck quits. Hen had a good plan. Now it is good to sit. Sit, sit, sit!

Duck and Hen will have fun. Hen trips, slips, and flips. Duck will, too. Trip, trip, trip! Slip, slip, slip! Flip, flip, flip!

64

61

Hen claps, flaps, and slaps. Duck will, too. Clap, flap, slap!

Hen flops, clops, and plops. Duck will, too. Flop, clop, plop!

TEKS **1.3A** decode words in context and in isolation; **1.3C(i)** decode using closed syllables

Phonics

Words with Consonant Clusters with l Read the sentences. Match the sentences with the pictures. Then point to and read words with clusters with l.

Fluff is a big black dog.

Does Glenn like to cluck?

Slim is a cat with a plan.

66

The Pet Club

by Ellen Catala

illustrated by Molly Delaney

Would you like to see pets?
Come to The Pet Club.

67

51B

Dom has a pet. His pet is Ham.
Ham can flip. Ham can flop.

Vocabulary

Read Together

Action Words

> flip   kick   run   sip   kiss

Act It Out   Work with a partner. Read the words. Then write each word on a card. Choose a card. Act out the word. See if your partner can guess the word from your actions. Then have your partner act out a word and you try to guess the action.

Nick has a pet. His pet is Plum.
Plum will not flip, flop, and clack.
Plum will not play, but Plum will kiss!

Roz has a pet cat. Her pet is
Glenn. Glenn can kick.

72

69

53B

Todd has a pet dog. His pet is
Slim. Slim can run. Slim can sit.

Ann has a pet. Her pet is Bluff.
Bluff can clack. Bluff can flap.

70

71

TEKS **1.3A** decode words in context and in isolation; **1.3C(i)** decode using closed syllables

Phonics

Words with Consonant Clusters with s Read each question. Find the picture that answers it. Then point to and read words that begin with a cluster with s.

What did Stan set up?

What did Skip pet?

What did Kim step on?

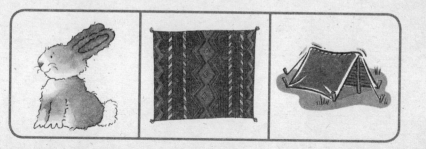

74

Step Up!

by Tanya Rivers

The clock struck 8.
We go to the bus stop.
Step up! Step up!

75

Can Jess read? Yes, Jess can!
Can Stan read? Yes, Stan can!

TEKS 1.4B ask questions/seek clarification/locate details about texts; 1.4C establish purpose/monitor comprehension ELPS 2I demonstrate listening comprehension of spoken English

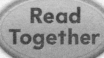

Use Strategies Read Together

Ask Questions To help you understand a story better, ask yourself questions as you read. Then read on to find the answers.

Read **Step Up!** on pages 75–80 again. If you do not understand a part or want to know more, ask yourself questions about the story. Then read the words and look at the pictures to find the answers.

Is it fun to step, step, step?
Is it fun to skip and sing?
Yes, it is! It is fun, fun, fun!

80

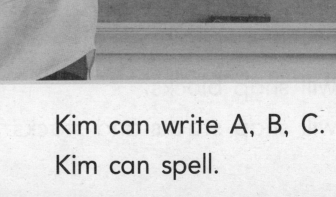

Kim can write A, B, C.
Kim can spell.

77

Jill will snap blocks.
Jill will snap stacks and stacks.

We pick a good spot.
Peg will spin. Bess will spin.
Jen will spin.

TEKS **1.3A** decode words in context and in isolation; **1.3C(i)** decode using closed syllables; **1.3E** decode words with inflectional endings

Phonics

Words with Consonant Clusters with s Read each sentence and find the matching picture. Then reread words that begin with a cluster with s.

Meg draws red spots.

Stan sleds on the hill.

Rex steps up.

82

62B

Splat! Splat!

by Svetlana Yarmey
illustrated by Rusty Fletcher

Meg has on a red smock.
Stan has on a tan smock.

83

Splat! Splat! Meg will draw spots. Meg will draw dots. What good pictures Meg has!

TEKS 1.3A(iii) decode words with consonant blends; 1.6A identify nouns/verbs; 1.6D categorize words; ELPS 1C use strategic learning techniques to acquire vocabulary

Words

Read Together

Verbs and Nouns Read these words.

> draw scraps smock snip trucks

Draw a chart like this one:

Actions	Things

Use the chart to sort the words from the box that name actions and words that name things. Add more words.

Meg will skip it.
Splat! Splat! Splat!

Snip! Snap! Stan will snip scraps.
Stan will snap blocks. What good
trucks Stan has!

Yum! Yum! Mom has snacks.
Stan will stop for a snack. Stan
has a big snack.

Stan has his snack. Yum! Yum!
Will Meg stop for a snack? Will
Meg skip her snack?

86

87

66B

TEKS **1.3A** decode words in isolation; **1.3D** decode words with common spelling patterns; **1.3E** decode words with inflectional endings

Phonics

Words with Consonant Clusters with <u>s</u> Read the words on each ladder. Tell which words rhyme. Tell what sounds are the same in the rhyming words.

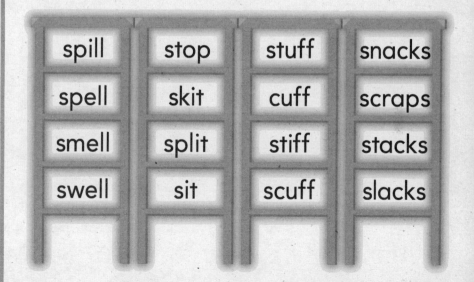

spill	stop	stuff	snacks
spell	skit	cuff	scraps
smell	split	stiff	stacks
swell	sit	scuff	slacks

90

68B

Miss Tess Was Still

by Ted Lutgen

illustrated by Mircea Catusanu

Miss Tess was still. Miss Tess was as still as a stick.

91

Now Miss Tess will skip.
Skip! Skip! Skip!

TEKS 1.17B develop drafts; 1.20A(i) understand/use verbs; 1.21B(ii) capitalize pronoun "I"; ELPS 5B write using new basic/content-based vocabulary

Writing

Read Together

Plan and Write   Read these words.

| skip | split | step | tap | spin |

Draw a picture of a way you like to move. Write a sentence that goes with your picture. Use a verb from the box.

Remember   Capitalize the word *I*.

Miss Tess has to stop. Miss Tess
will be still. Miss Tess will grin.
Click! Click! Click!

96

Miss Tess will do a split.
Split! Split! Split!

93

Miss Tess will step and tap.
Step! Step! Tap! Tap! Tap!

Miss Tess will spin. Miss Tess will
spin like a top. Spin! Spin! Spin!

94

95

Phonics

Words with Final Consonant Clusters

Read the words on the shells. Tell which words end with consonant clusters.

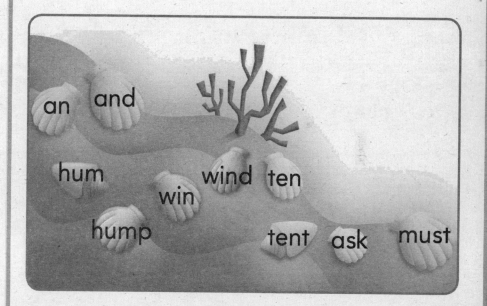

an   and

hum   wind   ten

win

hump   tent   ask   must

98

Who Likes to Jump?

by Cyrus Rivera

It is fun to jump. Gus and Liz
went to play. Gus and Liz run
and jump on a sand hill.

99

Fran will hop, jump, and land on 7. Next, Fran will hop, jump and land on 8 and 9.

TEKS 1.1B identify upper- and lower-case letters; 1.21B(iii) capitalize names of people

Letters

Identify Names

| Jill | hill | jump | Gus | hit |

1. Point to and read two names. What kind of letter do they begin with?
2. Point to and read the word that ends with a **t**. Is it a name? How do you know?
3. Which words are not names? How do you know?

It is fun to take small jumps and big jumps. Jump, jump, jump!

104

Jill will grasp the ends with her hands. Jill will jump as fast as she can. Jump, jump, jump!

101

Russ must jump and hit. Russ can jump up, up, up. Russ can hit. Russ can jump and hit.

Len is on a track. Len will run like the wind. Len will bend his legs and jump, jump, jump.

102

103

78B

TEKS **1.3A** decode words in context and in isolation; **1.3C(i)** decode using closed syllables; **1.3E** decode words with inflectional endings

Phonics

Words with Final Consonant Clusters Read each sentence. Tell which picture it goes with. Point to and read the words that end with consonant clusters.

Russ must rest.
Trent can jump in mud.
Grant will hunt for a nut.

106

The Lost Cat

by Jane Nicholas

illustrated by Kristen Goeters

"Mick!" said Bess. "Muff is lost!
Ask Trent to help us."

107

Trent is at his desk.

"Muff is lost? Yes! Yes! I will help," said Trent. "We must find Muff!"

TEKS 1.9A retell story events; 1.15B explain signs/symbols ELPS 3H narrate/describe/explain with detail; 4G demonstrate comprehension through shared reading/retelling/responding/note-taking

Retelling

Read Together

Events Think about these things from "The Lost Cat."

1. Trent's desk
2. the plant stand
3. Muff and her kits

Draw Make a map that shows these things. Draw cat tracks to show where Bess and Mick went. Use your map to retell the story to a partner.

82B

Muff is not lost! Muff has small
kits. Muff and her kits will rest
and rest.

Trent plans his task.
"Hunt," Trent said. "We must hunt
and hunt and hunt."

112

109

83B

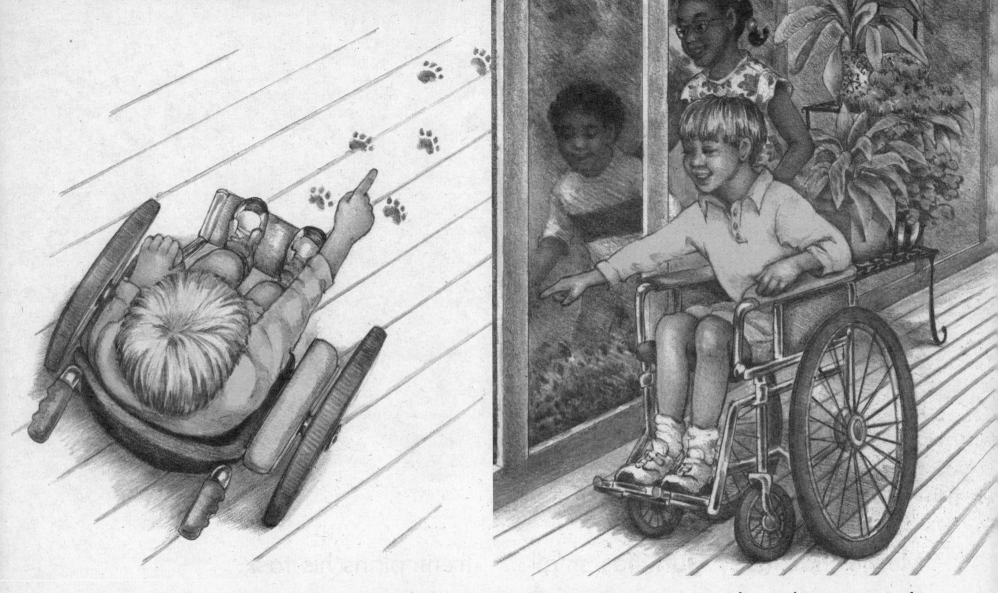

"Here is one hint. Cat tracks!
Tracks can take us to Muff."

Trent went past the plant stand.
At last, Trent can see Muff.

110

111

TEKS 1.3A decode words in isolation; 1.3C(i) decode using closed syllables

Phonics

Words with Final Consonant Clusters Name the pictures. Read the words. Name the pictures and words that rhyme. Use two rhyming words in a sentence.

plant	went
felt	ask
trust	bump
stamp	silk

114

86B

The List

by Ellen Catala

illustrated by Dorothy Donahue

"Take this list," Mom tells Brent.
"Run and get what is on the list."

115

List

Brent runs fast. Brent runs
too fast! He drops his list.

Use Strategies

Read Together

Ask Questions To help you
understand a story better, ask
yourself questions as you read.
Then read carefully to find the
answers.

Read **The List** on pages 115–120
again. If you do not understand
a part or want to know more,
ask yourself questions, such as:
**Why does Brent hunt for the
list on page 117? Does Brent
buy the right things?** Then
read the words and look at the
pictures to find the answers.

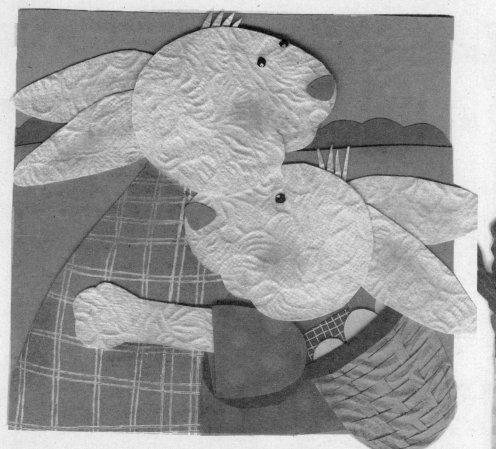

"I lost the list," Brent tells Mom, "but I got stamps, eggs, buns, nuts, and mints." "Brent is the best!" said Mom.

120

Brent is at the stand. Brent hunts and hunts, but his list is lost.

117

Brent gets stamps, eggs, and
buns. Brent gets nuts and mints.

Brent put the sack on his back.
Brent did not stop to eat a snack.

118

119

90B

Unit 3
Nature Near and Far

Contents

Phonics

Words with th Read each word. Tell which words have th. Use two th words in a sentence.

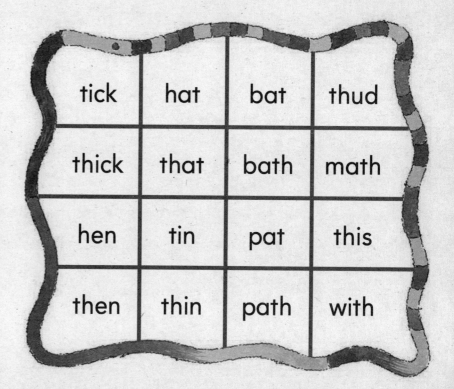

tick	hat	bat	thud
thick	that	bath	math
hen	tin	pat	this
then	thin	path	with

2

2C

Seth and Beth

by Anna Guzman

illustrated by Piero Corva

Seth and Beth met at the path.
Beth has a big map. It can help.
They will go and see Bob Frog.

3

This trip is far.
Seth and Beth pass Ben. Ben can see them. Seth tips his cap. Then Ben tips his cap.

Book Information

Read Together

Book Parts Remember that the **author** writes a story. The **illustrator** draws the pictures. The **title** is the name of the story.

Seth and Beth ← title
by Anna Guzman ← author
illustrated by Piero Corva ← illustrator

What is the title of this story? Who is the author? Who drew the pictures?

"Get up, Bob Frog!" Seth and
Beth call. "Play with us! This is
fun! It is fun."

This trip is far.
Beth and Seth pass Sam. Sam
can see them. Seth and Sam tip
their hats.

8

5

Beth and Seth pass Huck Duck.
They are at Blue Pond. Huck
can see them.
"Where is Bob Frog?" Beth yells.

"Does Bob Frog live here?"
Seth asks.
"Bob Frog is in this pond,"
Huck quacks.

6

7

6C

TEKS **1.3A** decode words in context and in isolation; **1.3C(i)** decode using closed syllables

Phonics

Words with <u>th</u> Read each sentence. Tell which picture goes with the sentence. Then point to and read the <u>th</u> words.

1. Jack has a thick pad.

2. Beth has a thin pen.

3. Rip gets a bath.

10

Zeb Yak

by Jane Tyler

illustrated by Katherine Lucas

This is Zeb. Zeb is a yak. Zeb is a little yak. Zeb is not big yet.

11

Zeb will get big and look like this.
Zeb will be like his big dad. Then
Zeb will go thud, thud, thud.

12

Fluency   Read Together

Words to Know Practice reading these words with a partner.

blue   cold   little   live

Read "Zeb Yak" with a partner. Take turns reading aloud. Read each word carefully. Check each other to see if you read these words correctly—<u>blue</u>, <u>cold</u>, <u>little</u>, <u>live</u>.

17

Zeb can look up. Zeb can see
lots of blue. Zeb can see the sun.
Zeb is one glad yak! Zeb will go
thud, thud, thud.

Zeb is with his mom. His mom will
eat grass. Zeb can eat grass.
Then Zeb and Mom will nap.

16

13

Zeb and his mom and dad live on this cold hill. Lots of yaks live with Zeb and his mom and dad. Yaks cut big paths on the hill.

Big yaks go thump, thump, thump.
Big yaks go thud, thud, thud.
The paths get big. No grass is on this yak path.

14

15

12C

TEKS **1.3A** decode words in context and in isolation; **1.3C(i)** decode using closed syllables; **1.3E** decode words with inflectional endings

Phonics

Words with <u>-s</u>, <u>-es</u>, <u>-ed</u>, <u>-ing</u>

Read the words in the box.
Use the words to complete the sentences.

quacks	resting	jumped	fixes

1. The cat is _____.

2. That pup has _____ up.

3. The man _____ a truck.

4. This duck _____ a lot.

Animal Moms

by James Wang

This mom has pups. She is resting on the rocks with them. Rest, pups. Rest, mom.

19

15C

This mom has cubs. The cubs are just like their mom. They can swim in this cold water! Swim, cubs. Swim, mom.

TEKS 1.14B identify important facts/details; **ELPS 1C** use strategic learning techniques to acquire vocabulary; **3D** speak using content-area vocabulary

Facts

Information from Text What important facts did you learn about animal mothers and babies from "Animal Moms?"

Share information Pick two animals you read about. Talk with a partner about how they are the same and different.

This mom is with her little ducks.

Ducks swim and swim. It is fun.

Have fun, ducks! Swim, swim, swim!

24

This mom is hunting with her cubs.

What is jumping in that water?

Hunt, cubs! Grab a snack!

21

17C

This mom is with her kits. They
swim in a pond. Their pond has
lots of sticks, grasses, and twigs.
Swim, kits. Swim, mom.

This mom is with her pups.
Their pond is filled with mud.
They can swim fast in wet mud.
Swim, pups. Swim, mom.

22

23

TEKS 1.3A decode words in context and in isolation; 1.3E decode words with inflectional endings

Phonics

Words with <u>ch</u> and <u>tch</u> Add the letters and read the words. Listen for the sound like the beginning of <u>chip</u>. Then read the sentences. Point to and reread words with <u>ch</u> or <u>tch</u>.

ch + at = <u>ch</u>at

ma + tch = ma<u>tch</u>

1. Chad and Van play catch.

2. Mitch chops
nuts for lunch.

26

Scratch, Chomp

by Edward Bonfanti

illustrated by Rick Brown

Chuck and his dad went off on a trip. At Finch Pond, Chuck and his dad played catch. Chuck has a fast pitch.

27

Dad can catch, but Dad did not catch this pitch.

"You never miss, Dad. Why did you miss?" Chuck asks.

Decoding

Read
Together

Read   Read carefully.

Can you hear <u>peck</u>, <u>peck</u>?
Does it <u>scratch</u>, <u>scratch</u>?
What animal can <u>peck</u> and
<u>scratch</u>? Is it a chick?

Think   Did you read every word correctly? If not, look again at the letters. Say the sounds the letters stand for. Now read the sentences again. Did you read the words better?

The bump has an animal on it.
This animal can scratch, scratch,
scratch. It can chop, chop, chop,
chop. It can chomp, chomp,
chomp. Can you tell what it is?

32

"I hear scratch, scratch, chomp,
chomp. Do you?" asks Dad.
"Yes! Scratch, scratch, chomp,
chomp. What is it?" asks Chuck.

29

Scratch, scratch, scratch. Chomp,
chomp, chomp. Can Chuck and
Dad find out what is scratching
and chomping?

30

Scratch, scratch, chomp, chomp.
Chuck and Dad can see a stump
and lots of chips. A big brown
lump is in the pond.

31

24C

TEKS **1.3A** decode words in context and in isolation; **1.3C(i)** decode using closed syllables

Phonics

Words with <u>ch</u> and <u>tch</u> Read each sentence and match it to a picture. Point to and reread words with <u>ch</u> or <u>tch</u>.

1. Chuck can stitch a patch.

2. A chick will scratch and peck.

3. Mitch and Beth like to sketch.

4. Chip and Chet munch lunch on a branch.

34

26C

Rich Gets a Dog

by Rick Eduardo

illustrated by Beth Spiegel

Mom and Dad tucked Rich in bed.
"Can I get a dog?" asked Rich.
"Hmmm," said Dad.
"Hmmm," said Mom.

35

Then Mom and Dad said yes.
Rich sat up in bed. Mom, Dad,
and Rich like dogs very much.

36

Writing Read Together

Ideas Draw pictures of
different kinds of dogs you
have seen.

Write Circle the dog you like
best. Write sentences that tell
what this dog is like.
    This dog is ____.
    This dog has ____.

41

Rich hugs Fletch. Fletch and Rich will be pals.

Today, Mom and Dad will get Rich a dog. Rich can see dogs, dogs, dogs. Rich can get just one dog.

Here are big dogs and small dogs. Here are fat dogs and thin dogs. Dogs, dogs, dogs!

Rich picks a brown dog called Fletch. Fletch is big and can run fast. Rich has his own dog!

38

39

TEKS **1.3A** decode words in context and in isolation; **1.3C(i)** decode using closed syllables

Phonics

Names and Words with '**s**

Follow the directions. Then point to and reread words with '**s**.

1. Find Mom's dog.

2. Find Dad's cat.

3. Where is Mitch's chick?

4. Where is Val's frog?

42

Kits, Chicks, and Pups

by Lara Heisman

Cats, dogs, and ducks have
moms and dads.

43

33C

Dog moms have pups. This mom and her pups sit still. They make such a good picture.

Speaking

Read Together

Share information Think about what you have learned about young animals. Share the information with a small group. Use these tips.

Speaking Tips

- Tell facts you have learned.
- Speak clearly and loudly enough to be heard.
- Do not speak too fast or too slowly.
- Use complete sentences.

This mom and dad know that chicks must eat. This mom's chicks will get fed. Mom and dad will do it. The chicks will get big.

48

Ducks do not have pups. Ducks have chicks. Ducks swim in a pond. Dad duck is with his chicks.

45

35C

This mom duck has a nest. Eggs will hatch in it. Chicks will pop out! Mom will get off the nest.

This kit can run. Mom cat will run, too. The kit and her mom will run and then stop and nap.

46

47

Phonics

Words with sh, wh, ph Read the sentences and match them to the pictures. Then point to and reread words with sh, wh, or ph.

1. You can see fish and shells.

2. I make a graph in math class.

3. Whack! Phil bats the ball.

50

Phil's New Bat

by Edward Bonfanti

illustrated by Jennifer H. Hayden

Phil's dad got him a new bat.
It was just what Phil wished for!

51

39C

When Phil got his new bat, he hit with it. When Phil got a hit, his bat went, "Wham! Bash!"

TEKS 1.4B ask questions/seek clarification/locate details about texts; ELPS 4G demonstrate comprehension through shared reading/retelling/responding/note-taking

Questions

Read Together

Ask Questions Ask yourself questions like these to better understand **Phil's New Bat** on pages 51–56.

- How did Phil feel when he got his new bat?

- What happened when Phil fell down?

- Why did Phil let his pal play with his bat?

Reread the story to figure out the answers. Share your ideas with a partner.

Phil's bat is in good hands.
Phil and his dad can play catch.
You do not catch with a bat!

56

Phil got many hits and runs. His
mom and his dad and his pal had
fun! Did Phil get a hit? Yes!

53

41C

Did Phil fall? Yes! Phil fell
down on his leg. Phil cannot
play with his bat for a bit.

Phil is not sad. If Phil cannot
play with his bat, Phil will let his
pal play with it.

54

55

Phonics

Words with sh, wh, ph Read all the words. Then find four words in a row that begin with wh and read them. Find four words in a row that end with sh and read them.

ship	graph	shop	shelf
when	which	whip	whisk
dish	crush	fish	splash
shed	wham	Phil	shell

58

43C

44C

In a Rush

by Sue De Marco
illustrated by Maria Maddocks

Shan is in a rush. She has to splash in cold, wet slush. She goes splish, splash, splish, splash.

59

Wham! Slip! Slop! Bash! Shan fell down in the wet slush. Shan just sat in slush. It felt like mush.

Retelling   Read Together

Discuss Plot   Talk with a partner about Shan's problem and how she solves it.

Write   Think about a problem you have had. Write a short story about how you solved the problem. Draw a picture to go with it.

Look at Shan! Shan is all in yellow. Slush is fun now. Shan is glad. Splish, splash, splish, splash, Shan!

Then Shan got up. Shan did not rush. Shan did not dash in the wet slush. Shan went plop, plod.

64

61

47C

Plop, plop, plod. Shan must get to Phil's Best Stuff Shop. That shop has lots and lots of stuff. Shan must get to that shop.

Phil's Best Stuff Shop is still open! Shan got to it at last. Shan will rush in. Shan has cash. What new stuff will Shan get?

62

63

48C

Phonics

Contractions Read the words and contractions. Then read the sentences. Tell what two words form, each contraction.

it + is = it's   **is + not = isn't**
he + is = he's   **did + not = didn't**

1. Where's Mom?
2. She's helping Phil.

3. That shell didn't crack.
4. The eggs aren't fresh.

66

Trish's Gift

by Bryn Haddock

illustrated by Mircea Catusanu

When Trish was ten, Gramps sent a gift. Trish and Mom opened it. It was a new desk.

"Dad," said Trish, "Gramps sent this desk with brass trim, but I can't sit at it."
"Let's see that desk with brass trim," said Dad.

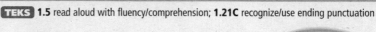

Fluency Read Together

End Marks Read these sentences from "Trish's Gift." Each sentence should sound different. Use the end marks to help you.

It was a new desk.
Where is that bench?
That's it!

Read Aloud Work with a partner. Use end marks to help you read aloud the story.

52C

"Did Gramps know that we had this bench with brass trim?" asked Trish.

"We can ask him," said Dad. "Let's call Gramps and ask."

"Back when I was just ten," said Dad, "I had a bench with brass trim on it. I got big, but that bench with brass trim didn't grow big."

"Where is that bench?" asked Trish.

72

69

53C

"Gramps put that bench in his shed," said Dad.

"Is that the shed Gramps had?" asked Trish.

"Yes, it's his shed," said Dad. Dad and Trish ran fast.

Trish and Dad hunted and hunted. Then Dad lifted up a big green cloth.

"That's it!" yelled Trish.

TEKS 1.3A decode words in context and in isolation; 1.3C(iv) decode using VCe pattern

Phonics

Words with Long a Read the words. Listen for the short a and the long a sounds. Then read the sentences. Point to and reread the long a words.

can + e = cane   mad + e = made

tap + e = tape   pal + e = pale

1. Let's bake a cake.

2. Jane ate some grapes.

3. Dave can wade in the lake.

74

Tate's Cakes

by Bruce Falcon

illustrated by Peter Grosshauser

Tate had never made a cake.
Tate did know that cakes must
bake. Can Tate make cakes?

75

"This sand is hot, hot, hot. Cakes can bake in it. What goes into cakes? If Wade has made cakes, Wade will tell me," said Tate.

TEKS 1.17A generate ideas for writing; 1.19A write brief compositions; 1.20A(iii) understand/use adjectives; ELPS 5B write using new basic/content-based vocabulary

Writing
Read Together

Plan to Write Look at Jade's cakes. Which one would you like to get? Draw a picture of it.

Describe Write sentences to tell your classmates about the cake. Use adjectives to tell how it looks, smells, and tastes.

Wade got four cakes. Tate got five cakes. Jade's bake sale was over. Tate and Wade ate Jade's cakes. Tate and Wade never did make cakes. They ate Jade's.

"Well, I never made a cake," said Wade. "Let's ask Jade. If Jade has made cakes, Jade will tell us."

"Yes," said Tate, "let's ask Jade."

Wade and Tate went to Jade's big
cave. Jade was in.
"I am glad you came," said Jade.
"I just made ten cakes."

"This cake is on sale. That cake is
on sale and that cake is on sale.
The big cakes are all on sale,"
Jade said. "I just made them."

78

79

TEKS 1.3A decode words in isolation; 1.3C(iv) decode using VCe pattern

Phonics

Words with Long a Read the words. Use one of the words in a sentence. Then use two of the words in a sentence.

whale	flake	tape
plate	wave	snake

82

62C

Dave and the Whales

by Andrew Hathaway
illustrated by Julia Woolf

Dave is a whale. Dave is fast.
"Let's play," Dave yelled. "Chase
me! Chase, chase, chase me!"

83

Dave's pals watch. Not one whale is as fast as Dave is. Dave did not get his pals to chase him. "Why chase Dave?" asked Jake. "We can't catch him."

Unit 3/Lesson 14/Selection 2

Words in Print

Read Together

Dialogue Print can show words people say. With two partners, read these sentences.

> **Dave:** "Let's go fast and make waves!"
>
> **Jake:** "I can't go fast, but I can sing."
>
> **Lane:** "I can't make waves, but I can sing."
>
> **Dave:** "Then let's all sing."

Act out what Dave, Jake, and Lane say with your partners.

"Sing, whales!" yelled Dave. "Let's make a tape. Let's name it Dave and the Whales! It will be a big hit!"

Dave made waves as big as hills. "Let's make waves!" yelled Dave. "Why?" asked Lane. "We can't make waves as big as Dave's." Dave did not get his pals to make waves.

88

85

Dave is sad. His pals will not play
with him.
"I get it," said Dave. "I am fast
and can make big waves. But, I
can't sing!"

"Let's sing!" yelled Dave.
Two whales came. Three whales
came. Then four and five whales
came.

86

87

66C

TEKS **1.3A** decode words in context and in isolation; **1.3C(iv)** decode using VCe pattern; **1.3D** decode words with common spelling patterns

Phonics

Words with Soft c and Soft g

Read each word pair. Say the sound for the underlined letter or letters. Is the sound the same or different in the two words?

<u>c</u>ent	pla<u>c</u>e	<u>g</u>em	bad<u>ge</u>
<u>s</u>and	ga<u>s</u>	<u>j</u>ump	pa<u>g</u>e

Read the sentence. Reread the words with underlined letters. Which stand for the same sound?

<u>M</u>a<u>dge</u> and <u>J</u>ane ra<u>c</u>e to the bu<u>s</u>.

90

The Race

by Carre Murray
illustrated by Jerry Smath

This race is fun to watch. Get into the fun! Yell, yell. Clap, clap. Race, race, race!

91

TEKS 1.3A(ii) decode words with vowels; 1.3D decode words with common spelling patterns; 1.6D categorize words; ELPS 4A learn English sound-letter relationships/decode

Spelling Patterns

Read Together

Sort Words Read the words:

race Trace late stage skate

Copy this chart.

_ace	_age	_ate

Write each word from the green box in the correct column. How are the words in each column alike? Add more words and read them.

Dave and Ace got in this race. Dave will run fast. Ace will run fast. Crack! The race starts. Dave and Ace take off.

92

97

70C

The last race is over. Madge,
Grace, Blake, Trace, Dave, and
Ace sit in the shade. The judge
gave two of them red badges
and four of them blue badges.

Dave has a lane. It is his space.
Ace has a lane. It is his space.
They must run and jump in that
lane. They can't trade lanes.

96

93

71C

Madge and Grace got in this race. They will skate fast. Go, Madge! Go, Grace! Skate as fast as you can. Race, race, race.

Blake and Trace got in this race. Blake and Trace set the pace. Will Trace race past Blake? Go, Blake! Go, Trace!

94

95

72C

TEKS **1.3A(i)** decode words in isolation; **1.3C(iv)** decode using VCe pattern; **1.3D** decode words with common spelling patterns

Phonics

Words with Long i Read all the words. Find three words with long i in a row. Reread those words. Then find and reread three words that do not have the long i sound. Tell what vowel sound those words have.

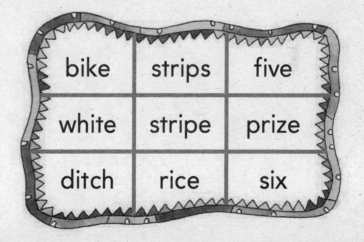

bike	strips	five
white	stripe	prize
ditch	rice	six

98

73C

Mike's Bike

by Claire Coolidge
illustrated by Jill Dubin

Mike's new bike is red and white.
Mike just got it. Mike can ride
it well. Mike rides his bike
with pride.

99

Mike will ride his bike to see Nell. His dad will ride with him. Nell will like Mike's bike. Nell's bike is red and white, too.

Vocabulary

Read Together

Verbs and Nouns Words that name actions are verbs. Nouns name people or things. Read these words.

| bike   ride   Mike   go   Dad |

Copy this chart.

Actions	People	Things

Write the words from the green box in the correct columns. Add more.

They stop at Nell's place.
"That was fun, Mike," said Nell.
Mike had a big, wide grin on
his face.
"Best time of my life!" said Mike.

Nell did like Mike's bike.
"I like its white stripes. Mine
has red stripes. Both bikes have
stripes," Nell said.

104

101

77C

Mike, Dad, and Nell take a ride. "This bike path is fun. I like it," said Mike. "It is nice to ride on." "I like it too," said Nell.

Dad, Nell, and Mike ride for five or six miles. It is a long ride. "This is the end," said Nell. "It is time to go back."

102

103

TEKS 1.3A(i) decode words in context and in isolation; **1.3C(iv)** decode using VCe pattern; **1.3D** decode words with common spelling patterns

Phonics

Words with Long i Read the questions. Point to and reread words with the long i sound. Then answer the questions. Use the pictures to help you.

1. What is black and white?

2. What can tell time?

3. What do mice like?

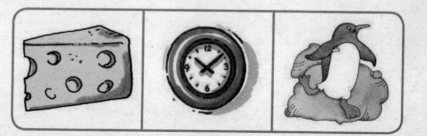

106

80C

The Nest

by Amy Long

This big bird has a name. His name is Pale Male. Pale Male's chest is white. Pale Male's neck is white.

107

81C

Pale Male has a nest. The nest is wide. It is a big, big nest. Pale Male made it. It can take a long time to make a big nest like this.

Retelling

Read Together

Order of Events Think about the story "The Nest." These story events are all mixed up.

- Chicks fly.
- There are eggs in the nest.
- Pale Male makes a nest.
- Dad and mom find mice for chicks.

Work with a partner. Retell the events in the correct order by using the words in the story.

This big chick can fly like Mom and Dad. This chick can rise up and dip down. Rise and dive, chick. Rise and glide, chick. Fly!

If you walk past it, look up. Pale Male's nest is not just a big pile of sticks and vines. It is a fine nest.

112

109

83C

The nest had eggs in it. It has small chicks in it now. Dad and Mom find mice for them. Those chicks get quite big, as big as Mom and Dad.

It is time to fly. Chicks grasp the nest at its side. Chicks flap and flap and flap. Then they let go and glide. Glide, flap, flap, glide. Both can fly!

Unit 3/Lesson 15/Selection 2

84C

TEKS **1.3A** decode words in context and in isolation; **1.3C(iv)** decode using VCe pattern; **1.3D** decode words with common spelling patterns; **1.3E** decode words with inflectional endings

Phonics

Words with <u>kn</u>, <u>wr</u>, <u>gn</u>, <u>mb</u>

Read the words. Use the words to complete the sentences.

write   knife   lamb   gnats

1. Cut the cake with this _____.

2. Some _____ can bite you.

3. I will _____ my name.

4. Mike has a pet duck and a pet _____.

114

Kite Time

by Zach Mathews

illustrated by Chi Chung

The wind is up. It's time to fly a kite. It's kite time! It's fun time!

115

A kite can ride on the wind. It can glide up on the wind. Wind takes a kite up and up. Wind can knock it down, too.

Unit 3/Lesson 15/Selection 3

TEKS 1.14B Identify important facts/details; 1.14D use text features to locate information; 1.24C record information in visual formats

Details

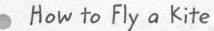 **Read Together**

Important Details With a partner, read "Kite Time" again. Look at the pictures. Identify important details in the text about how to fly a kite.

Together, make a list of important details about how to fly a kite.

How to Fly a Kite
1.
2.
3.
4.

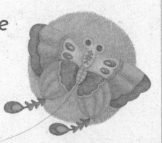

88C

If the wind stops, it's time to quit.
Wrap up the kites.

120

A kite can dip down. Then it can
rise back up. A kite can dip or
rise. It can rise, dip, and rise.
Wind can play with it.

117

89C

Make fists and run with the kite's line in them. Run with it. Run, run, run. Run fast! Then the kite will fly like a bird. Up, up, up it will rise.

It is up. Then it dips. It is up. Then it glides. It is up. Then it dives. It is up. Then it slides. Hold on to the kite's line. Do not let it go!

118

119

90C